Nonfiction Readers

We Help Out at School

By Amanda Miller

Children's Press®
An Imprint of Scholastic Inc.
New York Toronto London Auckland Sydney
Mexico City New Delhi Hong Kong
Danbury, Connecticut

These content vocabulary word builders are for grades 1–2.

Subject Consultant: Eli J. Lesser, MA, Director of Education, National Constitution Center, Philadelphia, Pennsylvania

Reading Consultant: Cecilia Minden-Cupp, PhD, Early Literacy Consultant and Author, Chapel Hill, North Carolina

Photographs ©2010: Alamy Images: 20 left, 21 top center (Blend Images), 10, 21 top left (Education Photos); Corbis Images/Jose Luis Pelaez, Inc.: 21 bottom right; Ken Karp: cover, back cover, 1, 2, 5, 6, 7, 8, 9, 11, 12, 13, 15, 16, 17, 19, 22 top, 22 bottom, 23 bottom, 23 top; PhotoEdit: 21 top right (Michael Newman), 20 bottom right, 21 bottom left (David Young-Wolff); The Image Works/Bob Daemmrich: 20 top right.

Art Direction, Production, and Digital Imaging: Scholastic Classroom Magazines

Library of Congress Cataloging-in-Publication Data

Miller, Amanda, 1974-
We help out at school / Amanda Miller.
    p. cm. – (Scholastic news nonfiction readers)
Includes bibliographical references and index.
ISBN 13: 978-0-531-21345-2 (lib. bdg.) 978-0-531-21449-7 (pbk.)
ISBN 10: 0-531-21345-5 (lib. bdg.) 0-531-21449-4 (pbk.)
1. Elementary schools–Juvenile literature. I. Title. II. Series.
LB1556.M55 2009   372–dc22   2009006422

CONTENTS

A Job for Everyone

Our classroom is a busy place. We all do our part so we can learn and play together every day.

We help out by doing our classroom jobs! Let's look at some of the jobs we do.

We are ready to do our jobs!

Jobs in the Morning

I am the pet and plant helper.

I feed our pet fish each morning. I water the plants with a **watering can**.

watering can

The fish is hungry in the morning!

I am the **calendar** helper. Each morning our class sits in a circle on the rug. I mark the date on the calendar.

I also give the **weather report**. I tell the class what the weather is like outside.

calendar

OCTOBER						
SUNDAY	MONDAY	TUESDAY	WEDNESDAY	THURSDAY	FRIDAY	SATURDAY
				1	2	3
4	5	6	7	8	9	10
11	12	13	14	15	16	17
18	19	20	21	22	23	24
25	26	27	28	29	30	31

I say, "The weather is cloudy today!"

9

Jobs All Day

I am the **office** helper. My teacher gives me a list of students who are in class today. I take it to the office.

Sometimes my teacher needs something from the office. I go pick it up.

office

OFFICE

ATTENDANCE

11

I am the paper passer. It is my job to pass out the work **folders** to the students.

I also collect the folders when we finish our work.

folders

Anna

MATH

13

I am the **line leader**. I go first when we line up.

We go many places. We go to the playground. We go to art class. We go to the lunchroom. I make sure our class walks quietly in the hallways.

line leader

I have my
☑ cub
☑ backpack
☑ book
☑ homework sheet

I ask, "Are you ready to go?"

I am the **caboose**. I also help when we walk in a line. I go at the end, like the caboose on a train.

I turn off the lights when we leave the classroom. I make sure the door is shut.

caboose

I like going last when it is my job!

One Last Job

We clean up at the end of the day. It is a big job, so we all work together!

We make sure there is no trash on the floor. We push in our chairs. We erase the board, too.

What jobs do you do in *your* classroom?